I0559702

16 Cross Stitch Easter Patterns

by Kay Goodnight

ISBN 978-1-958494-10-3

About the Author

Kay Goodnight enjoys crafts of all kinds – cross stitch, crochet, jewelry making, and water color painting among others. She has also published several books for children including PETDEMONIUM (books 1 and 2), MISTWIZZLED, SIDEWAYS WISHES and THE ADVENTURES OF PB AND JAY, a series for early readers.

Kay's other cross stitch books include:

> Small Christmas Cross Stitch Ornaments
> Gnomes for the Holidays
> Cross Stitch Cats

Table on Contents

For Your Reference

Color images for each project are on the front and back covers.

Basic Supplies

Each project requires the same basic supplies.

Embroidery Hoop (optional)

- A 4" hoop works well for the designs in this book. However, hoops come in a large variety of sizes to fit your needs.

Embroidery Thread (Floss)

- In this book, there are 4 to 16 colors per pattern.

- The DMC floss colors and numbers are listed with each pattern.

- Colors are repeated from one pattern to the next to help provide a cohesive look from project to project. It also allows stitchers to utilize the same colors purchased for more than one pattern.

Scissors

Cross Stitch Needle

- These have a larger loop for threading the floss and duller tip than other needles since the fabric used already has holes.

Fabric

- Using Aida 14 count fabric will result in a finished project the same approximate size as indicated on each of the patterns in this book. However, these patterns can be used with larger or smaller count fabrics as well as with plastic canvas.

General Information

- The larger patterns in this book (1 through 6) are shown two ways: once *without* the backstitching and once *with* the backstitching. If the backstitching lines cover up a floss color code, stitchers can refer to the pattern without backstitching for assistance.

- Details provided for each pattern include:
  - the finished size,
  - number of floss colors required,
  - number of stitches for the project,
  - floss color codes,
  - and backstitching details.

1 - Chick in a Nest

General Information

Fabric count: 14 count Aida

Stitches: 42 by 42

Total skeins: 12

Finished size: 3" by 3"

Total Stitches: 1,191

Floss type: DMC

DMC Embroidery Floss Color Code

⇥	D05	Driftwood LT	Stitches: 112
▼	D07	Driftwood	Stitches: 84
◁	D08	Driftwood DK	Stitches: 78
μ	D310	Black	Stitches: 6
□	D605	Cranberry VY LT	Stitches: 44
↗	D731	Olive Green DK	Stitches: 204
L	D734	Olive Green LT	Stitches: 248
R	D741	Tangerine MD	Stitches: 43
Y	D742	Tangerine LT	Stitches: 55
◖	D743	Pale Yellow	Stitches: 189
◣	D745	Pale Yellow LT	Stitches: 62
B	D3713	Salmon VY LT	Stitches: 66

Back Stitching

Basket weaving details: D08 Driftwood DK

Pink flowers' veins: D605 Cranberry VY LT

Flower stems and leaf details: D731 Olive Green DK

Duck's bill: D741 Tangerine MD

Duck's outline: D745 Pale Yellow LT

Chick in a Nest (Without Backstitching)

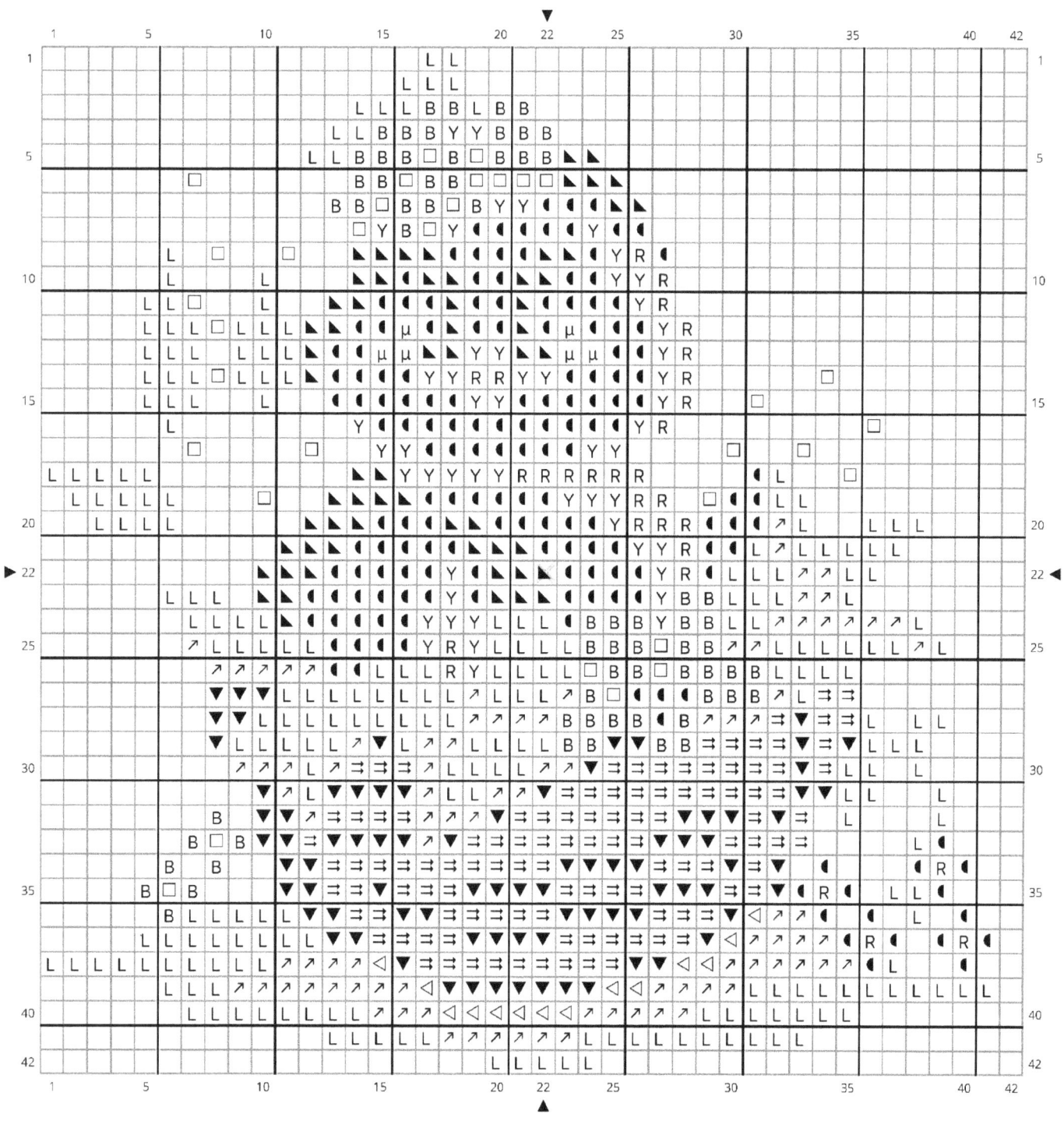

Chick in a Nest (WITH Backstitching)

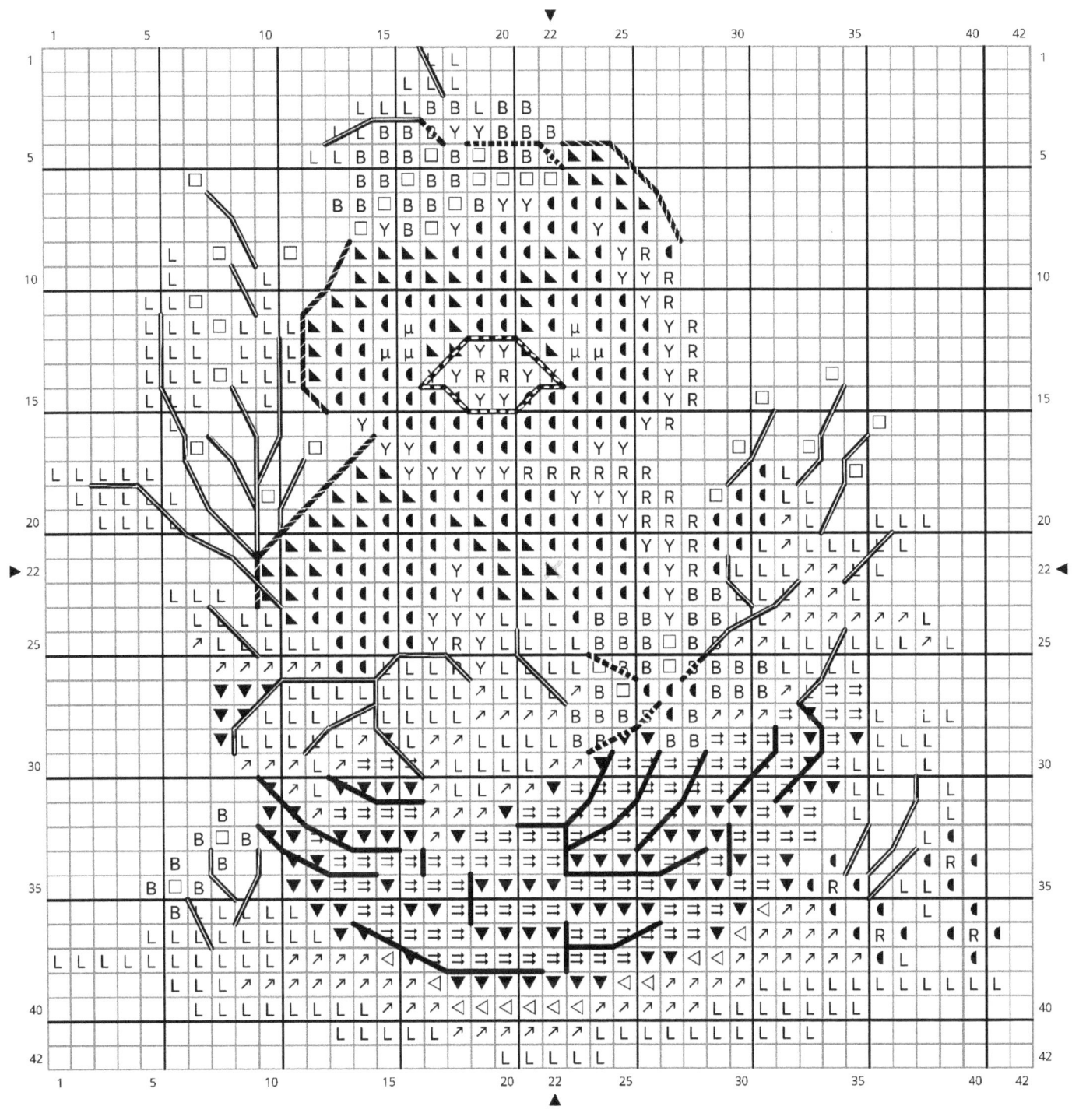

2 - Brown Bunny

General Information

Fabric count: 14 count Aida

Stitches: 40 by 42

Total skeins: 13

Finished size: 2.8" by 3"

Total Stitches: 1,088

Floss type: DMC

DMC Embroidery Floss Color Code

P	D210	Lavender MD	Stitches: 18
L	D211	Lavender LT	Stitches: 37
▲	D310	Black	Stitches: 13
←	D731	Olive Green DK	Stitches: 73
V	D734	Olive Green LT	Stitches: 118
♡	D738	Tan VY LT	Stitches: 97
⇐	D739	Tan UL VY LT	Stitches: 160
⇨	D742	Tangerine LT	Stitches: 41
◖	D743	Pale Yellow	Stitches: 95
◉	D948	Peach VY LT	Stitches: 32
Q	D3856	Mahogany UL VY LT	Stitches: 55
▣	DBLANC	White	Stitches: 53
↻	DECRU	Off-White	Stitches: 296

Back Stitching

Lavender flower petal highlights: D210 Lavender MD

Leaf veins and grass: D731 Olive Green DK

Inside the orange part of each flower: D734 Olive Green LT

Paws' toes: D738 Tan VY LT

Single stitches on either side of nose: D739 Tan UL VY LT

Yellow flower petal highlights: D742 Tangerine LT

Across tops of both ears; the left yellow flower additional petal highlights: D948 Peach VY LT

Eye highlights: DBLANC White

Brown Bunny (Without Backstitching)

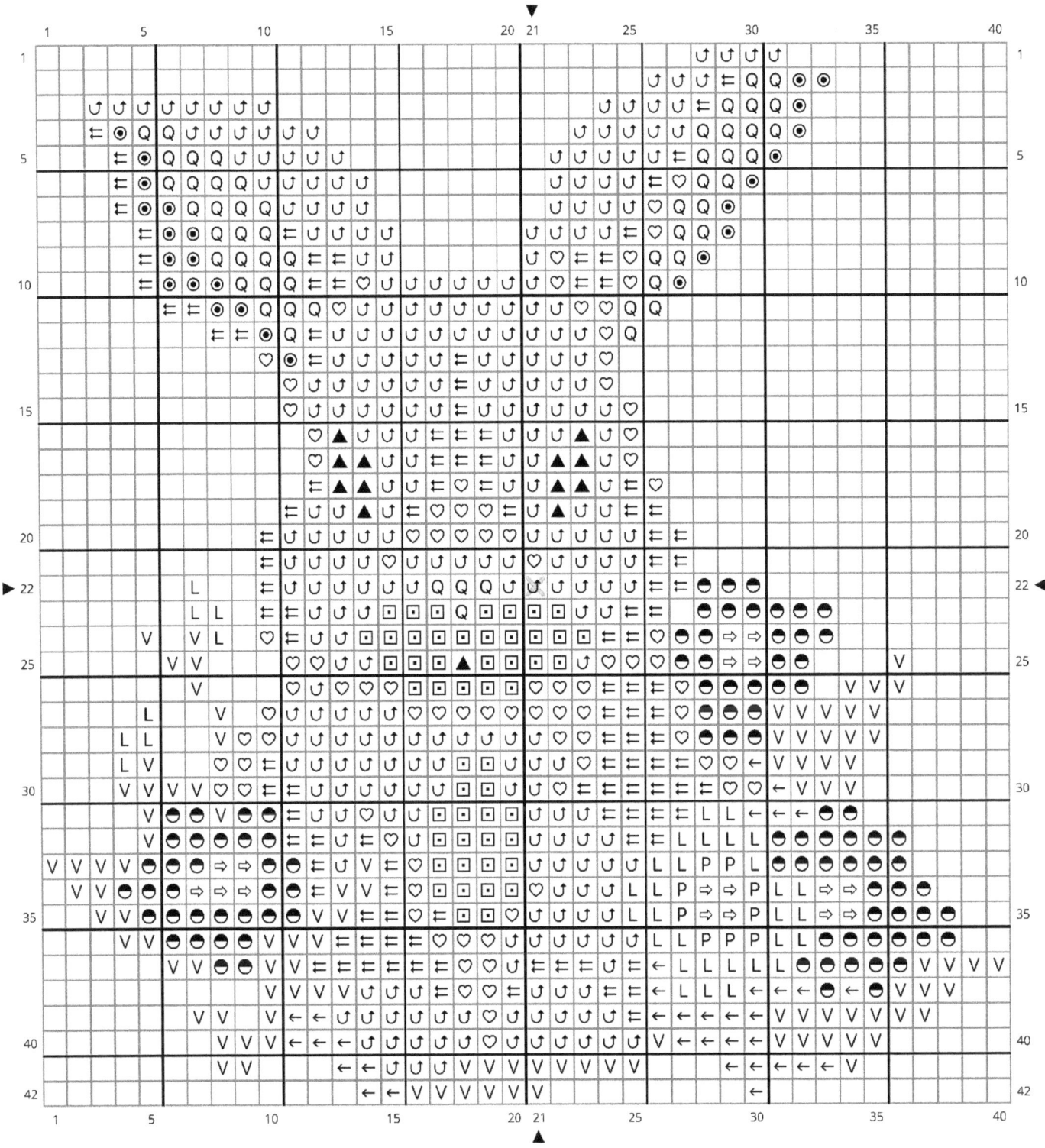

Brown Bunny (WITH Backstitching)

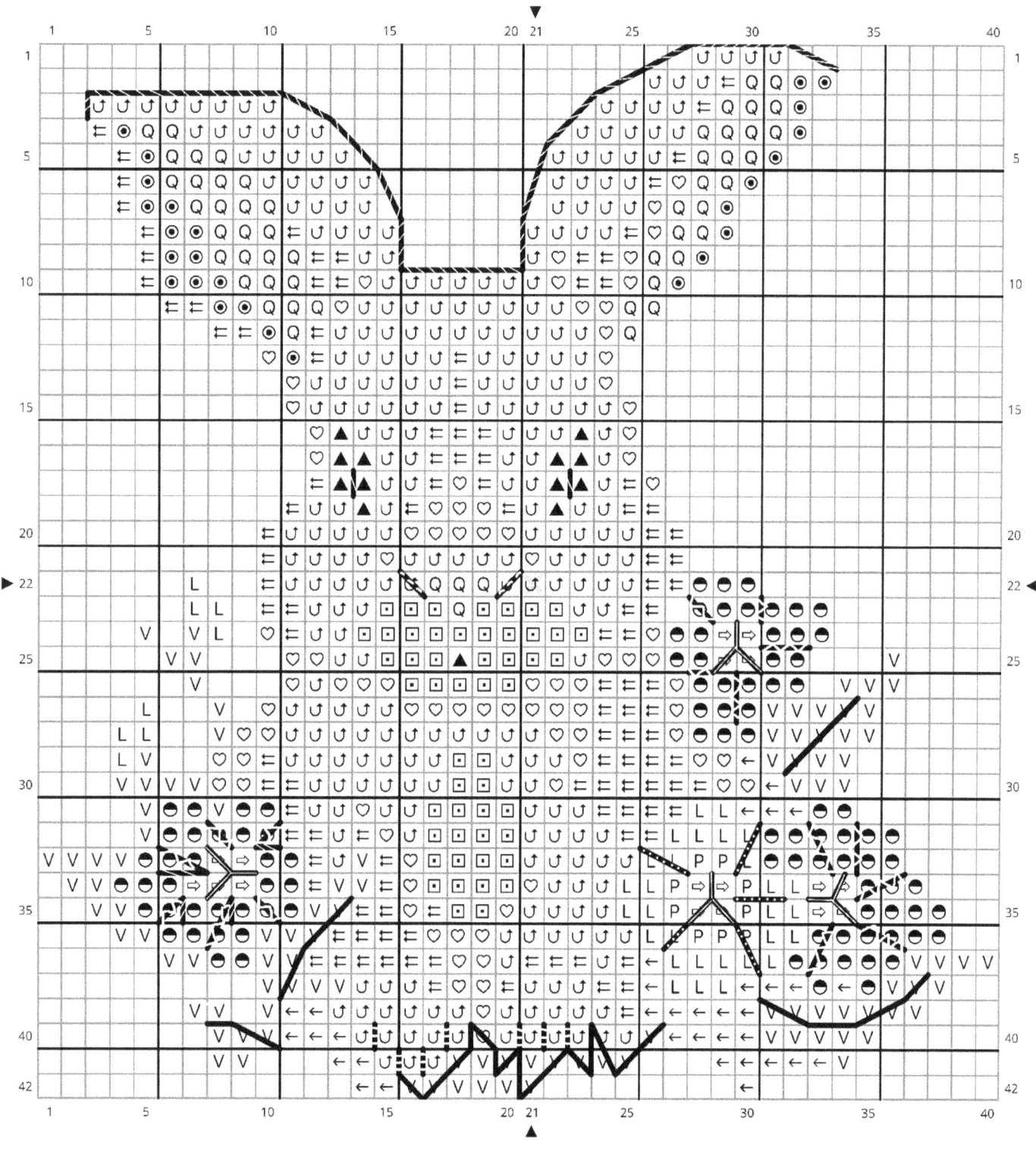

3 - Chick in a Spring Bonnet

General Information

Fabric count: 14 count Aida

Stitches: 41 by 42

Total skeins: 14

Finished size: 2.9" by 3"

Total Stitches: 1,670

Floss type: DMC

DMC Embroidery Floss Color Code

⚡	D310	Black	Stitches: 6
←	D731	Olive Green DK	Stitches: 43
◆	D734	Olive Green LT	Stitches: 63
↖	D741	Tangerine MD	Stitches: 292
⇥	D742	Tangerine LT	Stitches: 111
⇆	D743	Pale Yellow	Stitches: 190
↻	D745	Pale Yellow LT	Stitches: 86
φ	D746	Off White	Stitches: 178
↻	D3608	Plum VY LT	Stitches: 108
▶	D3713	Salmon VY LT	Stitches: 169
↶	D3810	Turquoise DK	Stitches: 139
Q	D3811	Turquoise VY LT	Stitches: 115
Z	DBLANC	White	Stitches: 68

Floss Color Only Used for Backstitching

D01 White Tin

Back Stitching

/ **White bonnet lace highlights**: D01 White Tin

/ **Leaf veins and stems**: D731 Olive Green DK

// **Beak, yellow flower outlines, chick's feet, stipes on turquoise egg**: D741 Tangerine MD

/ **Outline of left side of chick, stripes on turquoise egg**: D743 Pale Yellow

/ **Pink zig zag on left egg, pink flowers and ribbon outlines**: D3608 Plum VY LT

/ **Stripes on dark turquoise egg**: D3713 Salmon VY LT

/ **Blue flower outlines and left inside of bonnet**: D3810 Turquoise DK

/ **Stripes on dark durquoise egg**: D3811 Turquoise VY LT

Chick in a Spring Bonnet (Without Backstitching)

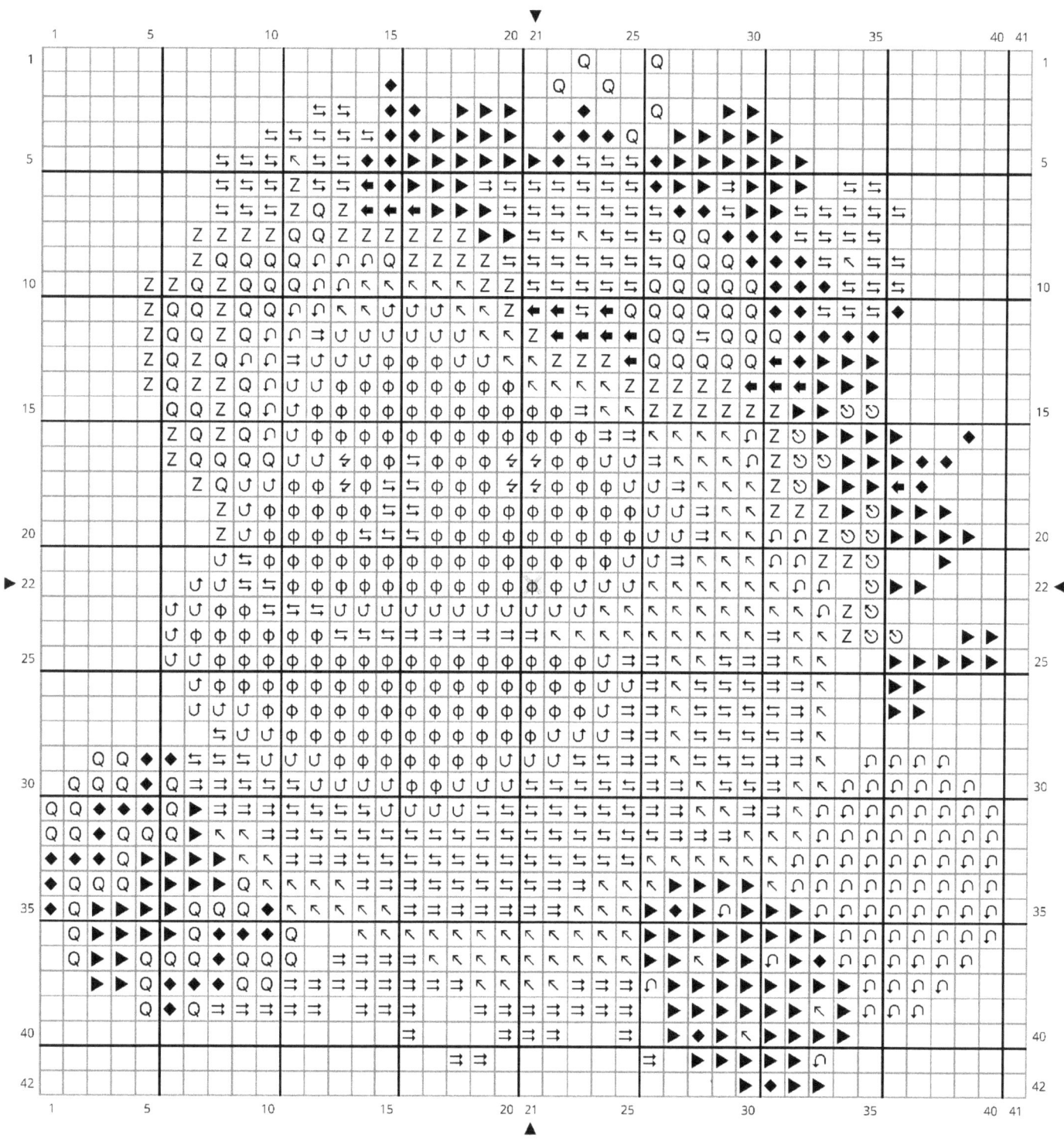

Chick in a Spring Bonnet – (With Backstitching)

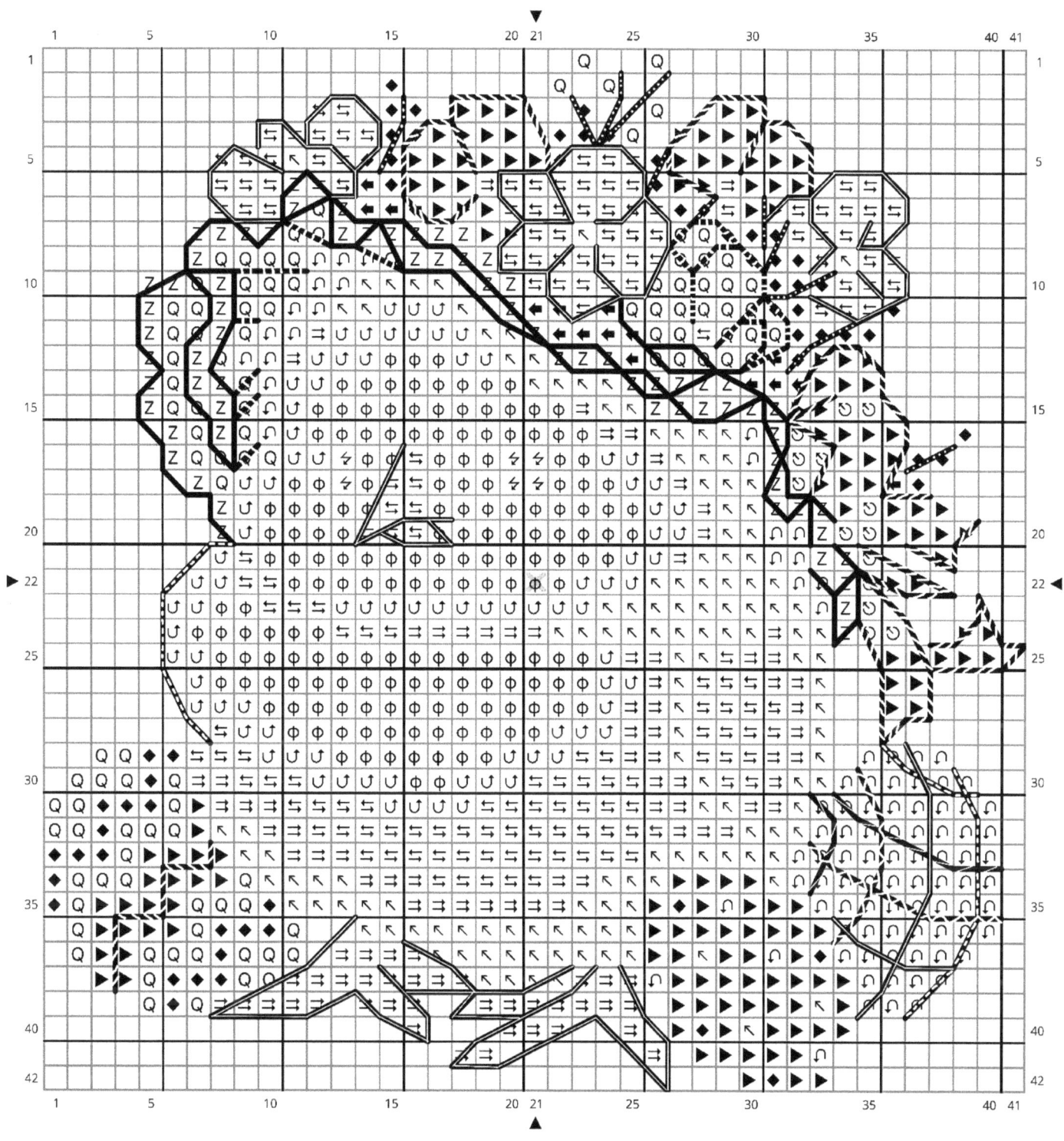

4 - Gray Easter Bunny

General Information

Fabric count: 14 count Aida

Stitches: 39 by 42

Total skeins: 14

Finished size: 2.7" by 3"

Total Stitches: 1,228

Floss type: DMC

DMC Embroidery Floss Color Code

⇐	D01	White Tin	Stitches: 280
▲	D02	Tin	Stitches: 124
♡	D03	Tin MD	Stitches: 51
☽	D04	Tin DK	Stitches: 118
↺	D211	Lavender LT	Stitches: 71
◀	D310	Black	Stitches: 6
↕	D731	Olive Green DK	Stitches: 66
↗	D734	Olive Green LT	Stitches: 104
▶	D743	Pale Yellow	Stitches: 90
↩	D948	Peach VY LT	Stitches: 56
↗	D3811	Turquoise VY LT	Stitches: 158
◗	DBLANC	White	Stitches: 65

> **Floss Colors Only Used for Backstitching**
>
> D210 Lavender MD
>
> D3810 Turquoise DK

Back Stitching

- **Top of ears, sides of face, paws, tail:** D03 Tin MD
- **Eyebrows, outline of eyes, paws' toes:** D04 Tin DK
- **Petals of lavender flower, outline of lavender parts of egg:** D210 Lavender MD
- **Line under foot:** D731 Olive Green DK
- **'Y' at center of both flowers:** D734 Olive Green LT
- **Outline of yellow parts of egg:** D743 Pale Yellow
- **Underside of ears, mouth:** D948 Peach VY LT
- **Petals of blue flower, outline of blue parts of egg:** D3810 Turquoise DK

Gray Easter Bunny (Without Backstitching)

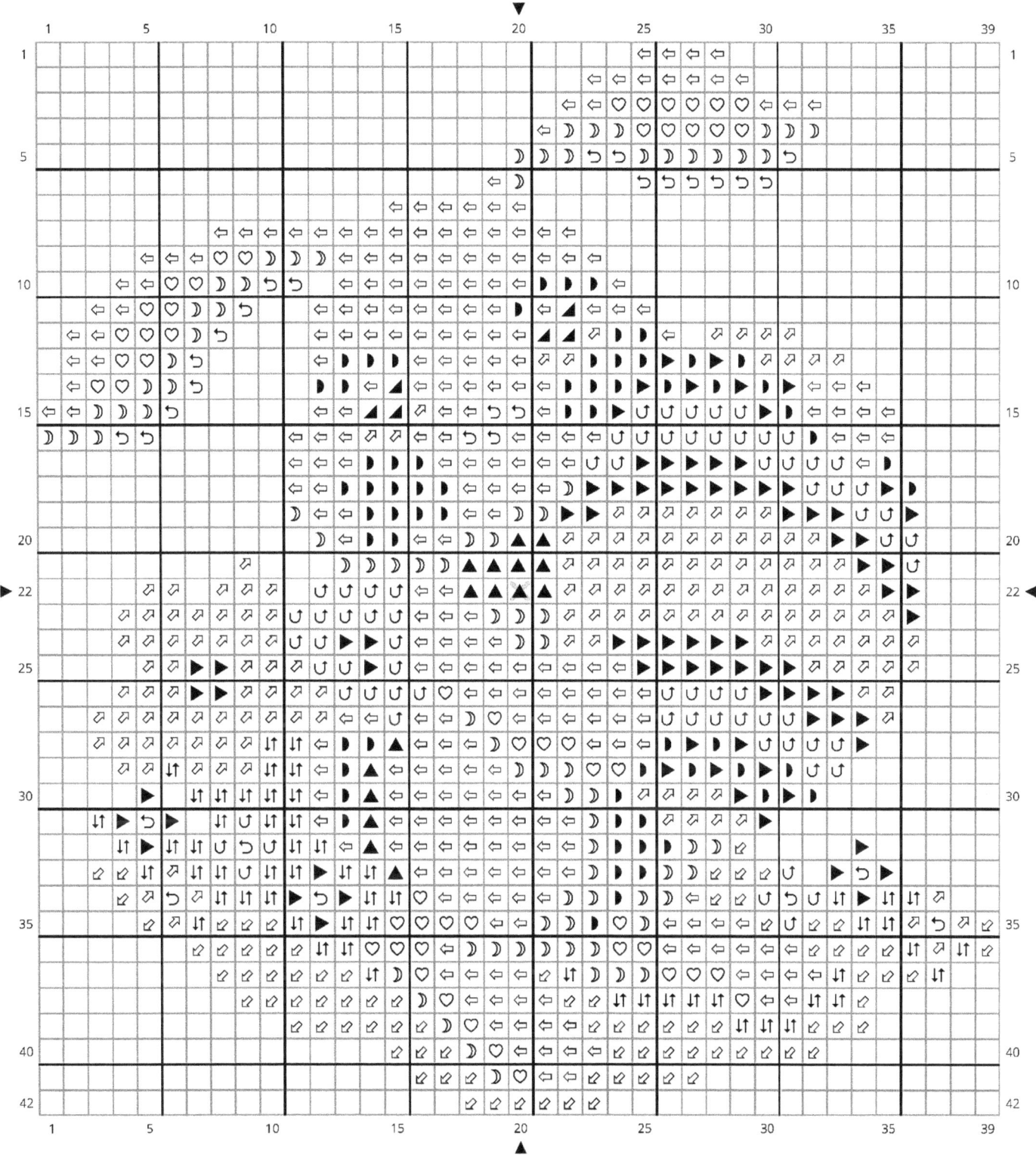

Gray Easter Bunny (WITH Backstitching)

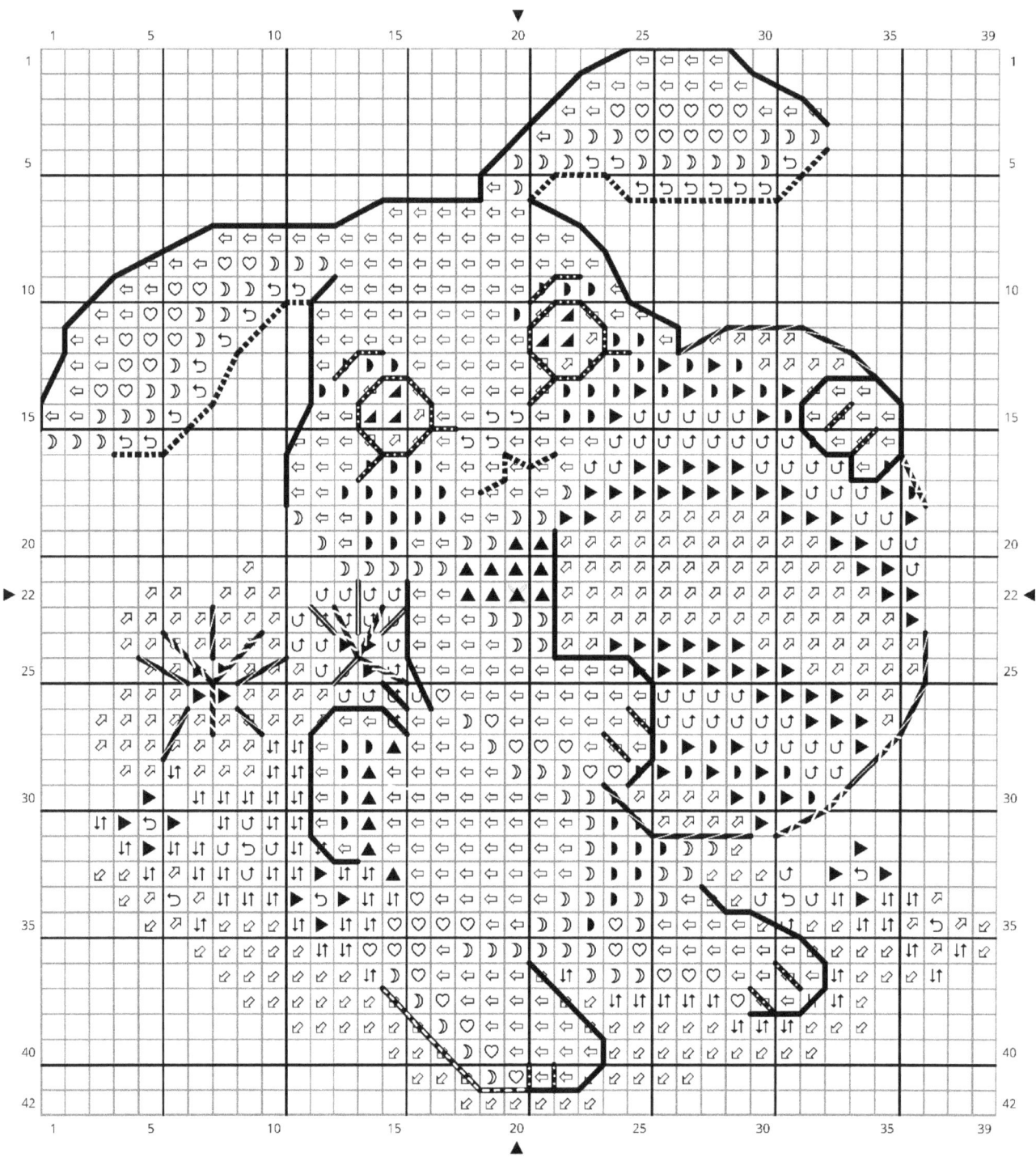

5 – "Hoppy Easter"

General Information

Fabric count: 14 count Aida

Stitches: 55 by 45

Total skeins: 11

Finished size: 4.1" by 3.2"

Total Stitches: 1,809

Floss type: DMC

DMC Embroidery Floss Color Code

E	D208	Lavender VY DK	Stitches: 159
θ	D211	Lavender LT	Stitches: 180
◄	D734	Olive Green LT	Stitches: 138
Q	D742	Tangerine LT	Stitches: 239
φ	D743	Pale Yellow	Stitches: 198
I	D3713	Salmon VY LT	Stitches: 234
◇	D3811	Turquoise VY LT	Stitches: 157
↘	DECRU	Off-White	Stitches: 14

Floss Colors Only Used for Backstitching

D741 Tangerine MD

D3608 Plum VY LT

D3810 Turquoise DK

Back Stitching

Outline of "H" and large butterfly: D208 Lavender VY DK

Outline of "o", "t", and small butterfly: D3810 Turquoise DK

Outline of first "p", "y", "a", and "e": D742 Tangerine LT

Line in interior of "o": D3713 Salmon VY LT

Outline and stripes of second "p", "E", "r", and outline of flower: D3608 Plum VY LT

Zigzag on interior of "o": D743 Pale Yellow

Vines: D734 Olive Green LT

Hoppy Easter (Without Backstitching)

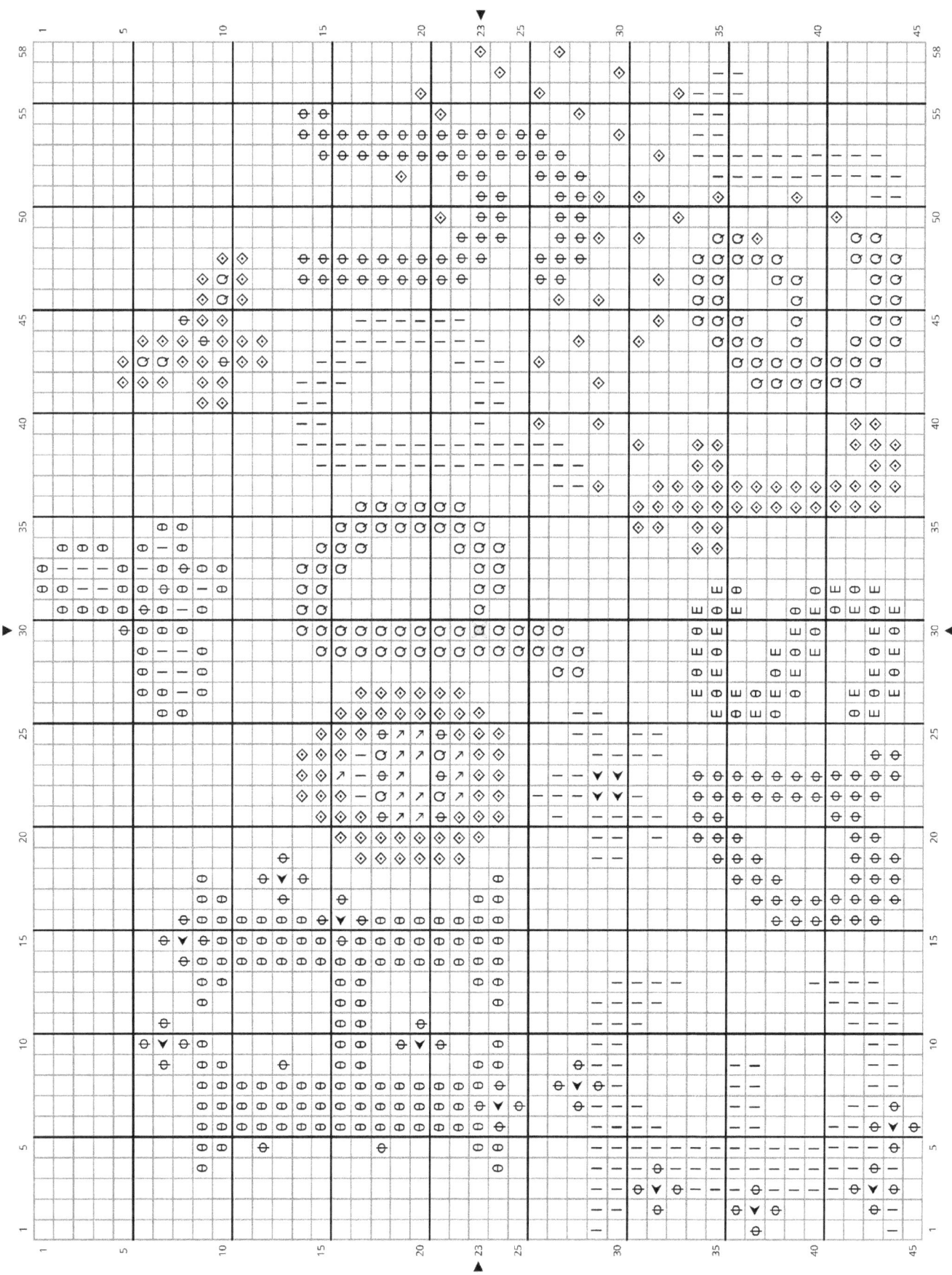

18

6 - Napping Bunny

General Information

Fabric count: 14 count Aida

Stitches: 45 by 40

Total skeins: 16

Finished size: 3.2" by 2.8"

Total Stitches: 1,621

Floss type: DMC

DMC Embroidery Floss Color Code

↻	D01	White Tin	Stitches: 40
■	D02	Tin	Stitches: 147
π	D05	Driftwood LT	Stitches: 249
&	D07	Driftwood	Stitches: 123
◗	D211	Lavender LT	Stitches: 70
◢	D731	Olive Green DK	Stitches: 74
N	D734	Olive Green LT	Stitches: 234
⇦	D742	Tangerine LT	Stitches: 42
▶	D743	Pale Yellow	Stitches: 129
B	D3713	Salmon VY LT	Stitches: 93
Z	D3811	Turquoise VY LT	Stitches: 85
△	DBLANC	White	Stitches: 180

Floss Colors Only Used for Backstitching

D08 Driftwood DK

D210 Lavender MD

D310 Black

D3810 Turquoise DK

Back Stitching

Outline of Bunny, paws: D02 Tin

Basket: D07 Driftwood

Basket: D08 Driftwood DK

Purple flowers' petals highlights: D210 Lavender MD

Eyes: D310 Black

Blue flowers' stems at the right side, short center lines inside bottom yellow flower: D734 Olive Green LT

Long lines inside yellow flowers: D742 Tangerine LT

Mouth: D3713 Salmon VY LT

Blue flowers' petals highlights: D3810 Turquoise DK

Napping Bunny (Without Backstitching)

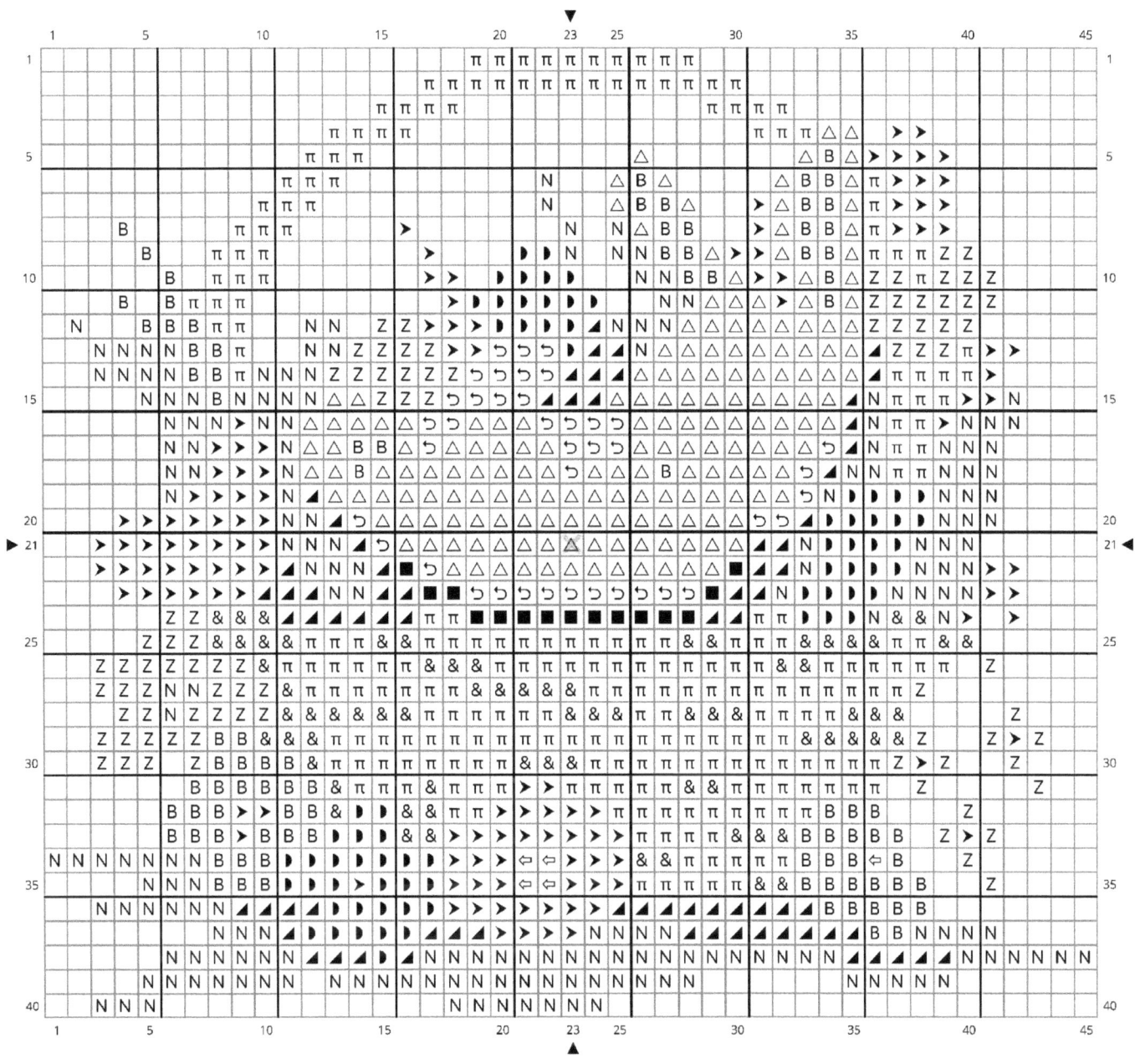

Napping Bunny (WITH Backstitching)

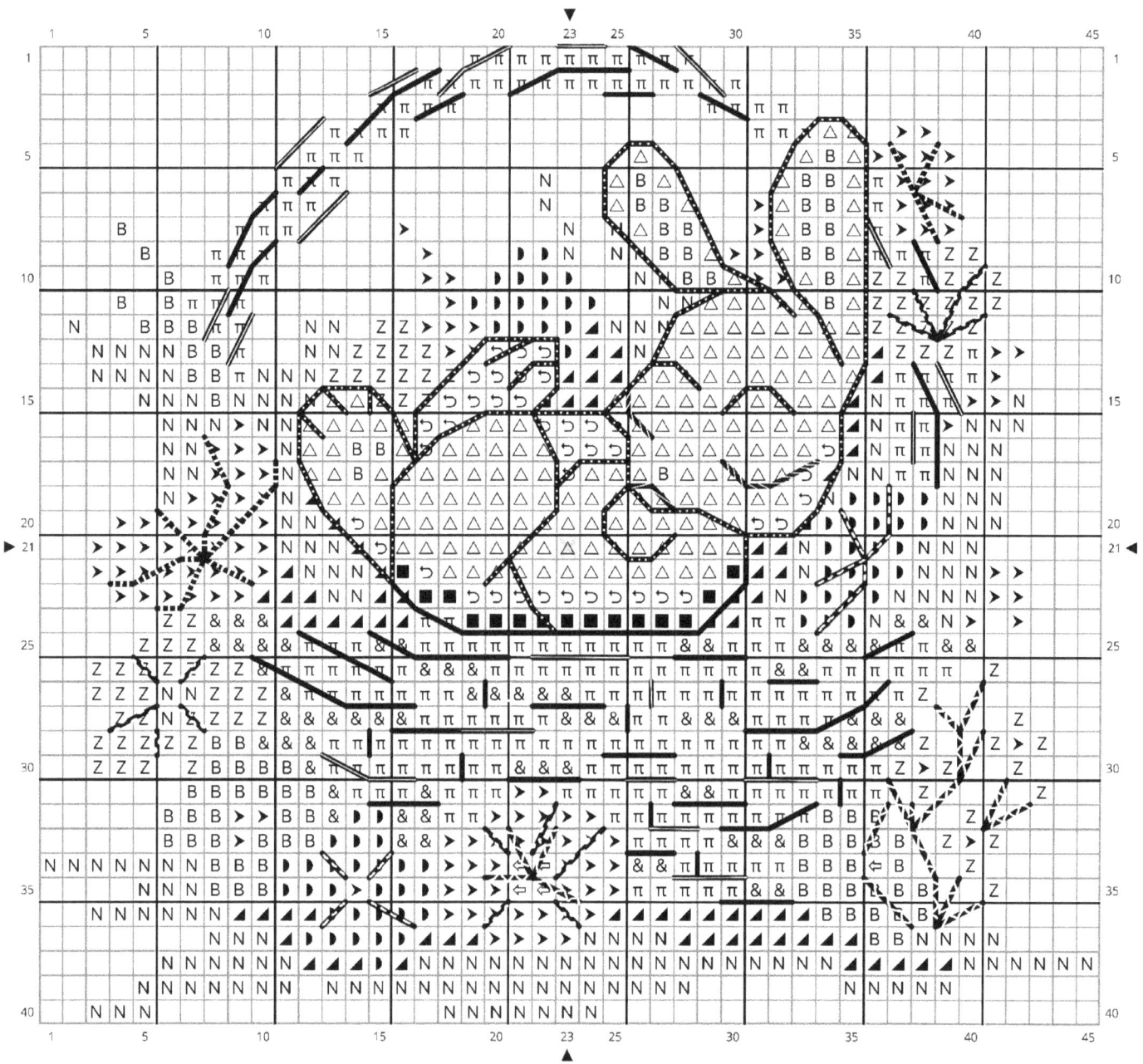

7 - Rainbow Easter Egg

General Information

Fabric count: 14 count Aida

Stitches: 19 by 24

Total skeins: 6

Finished size: 1.3" by 1.7"

Total Stitches: 353

Floss type: DMC

DMC Embroidery Floss Color Code

δ	D16	Chartreuse LT	Stitches: 72
◁	D210	Lavender MD	Stitches: 32
☆	D307	Lemon	Stitches: 82
%	D740	Tangerine	Stitches: 67
λ	D891	Carnation DK	Stitches: 54
◖	D996	Electric Blue MD	Stitches: 46

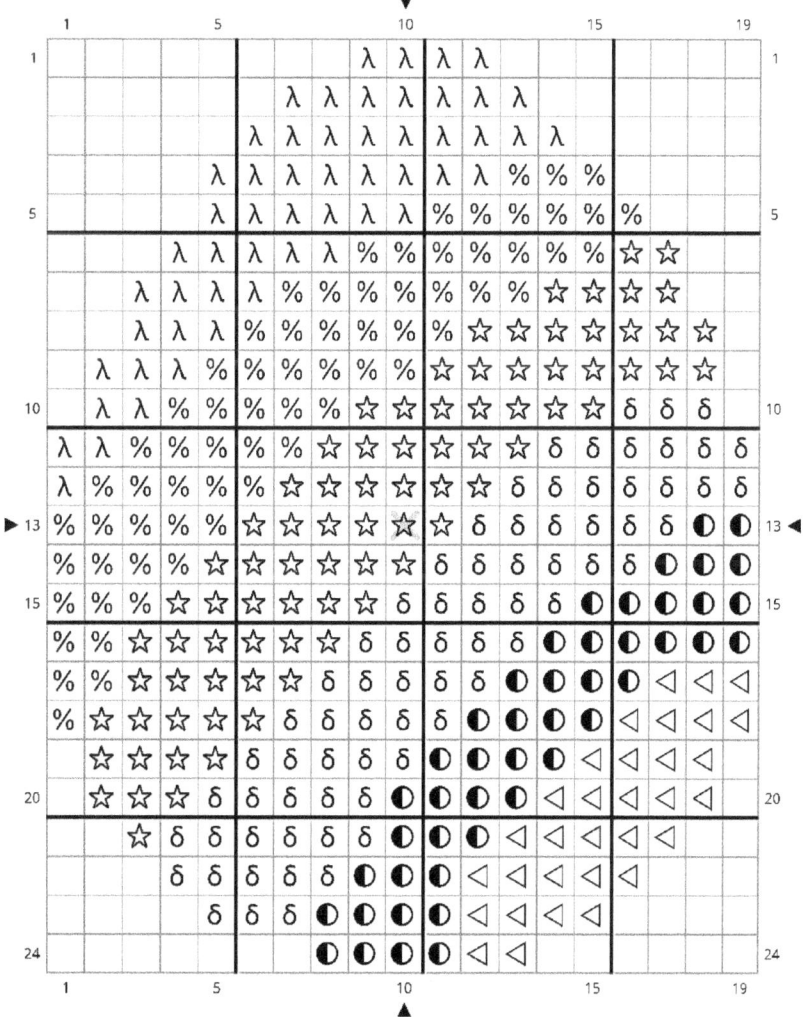

8 - Three Bunnies

General Information

Fabric count: 14 count Aida

Stitches: 28 by 17

Total skeins: 4

Finished size: 2" by 1.2"

Total Stitches: 284

Floss type: DMC

DMC Embroidery Floss Color Code

☆	D307	Lemon	Stitches: 83
△	D907	Parrot Green LT	Stitches: 82
♡	D957	Pale Geranium	Stitches: 83
◉	DBLANC	White	Stitches: 36

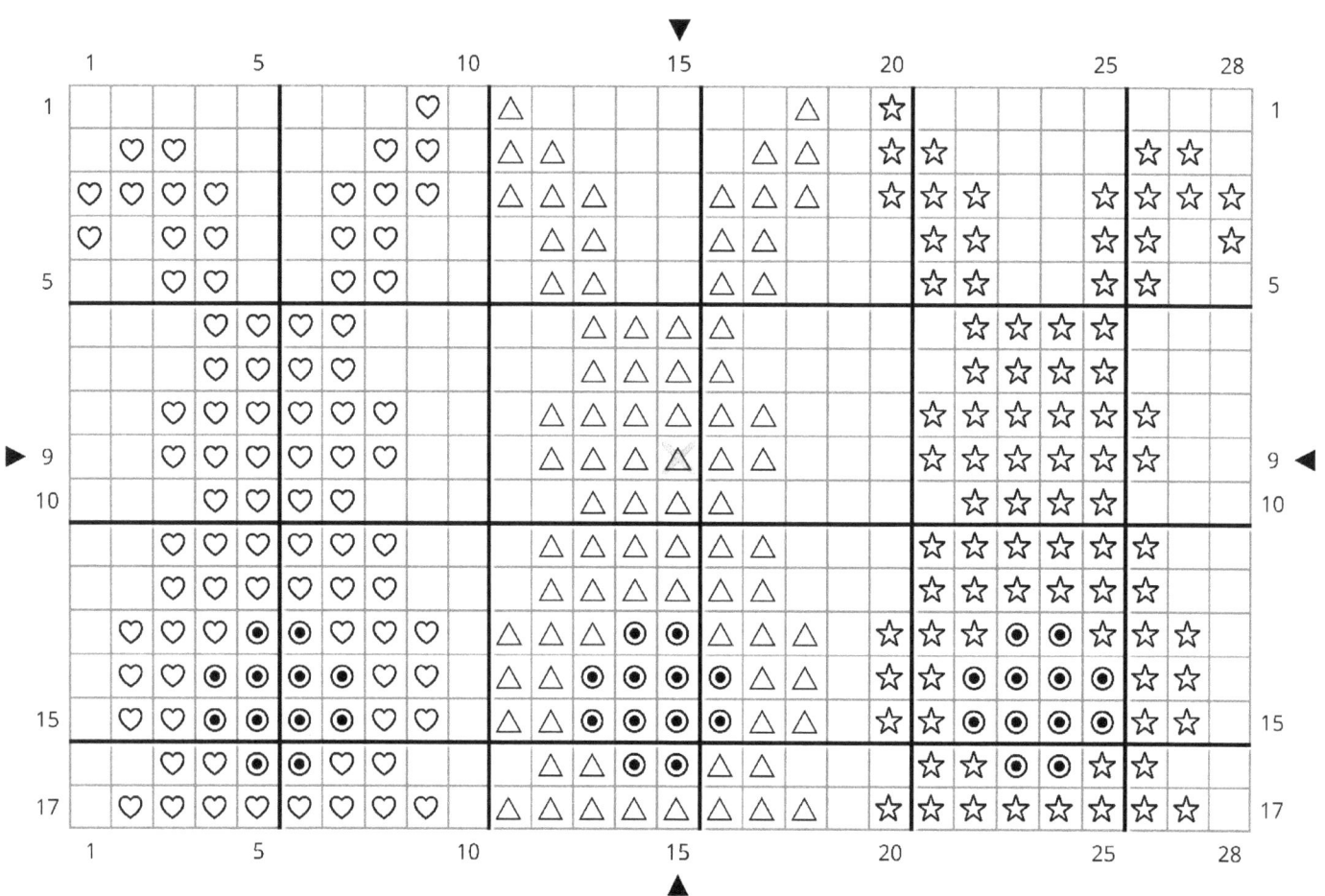

9 - Hatching Chick

General Information

Fabric count: 14 count Aida

Stitches: 18 by 24

Total skeins: 7

Finished size: 1.2" by 1.7"

Total Stitches: 326

Floss type: DMC

DMC Embroidery Floss Color Code

λ	D19	Autumn Gold MD LT	Stitches: 26
╱	D19	Autumn Gold MD LT	Stitches: 28 backstitching
☆	D307	Lemon	Stitches: 116
▼	D310	Black	Stitches: 6
€	D740	Tangerine	Stitches: 4
⊖	D891	Carnation DK	Stitches: 18
♥	D894	Carnation VY LT	Stitches: 126
⊙	DBLANC	White	Stitches: 2

Back Stitching:

Outline of baby chick:

D19 Autumn Gold MD LT

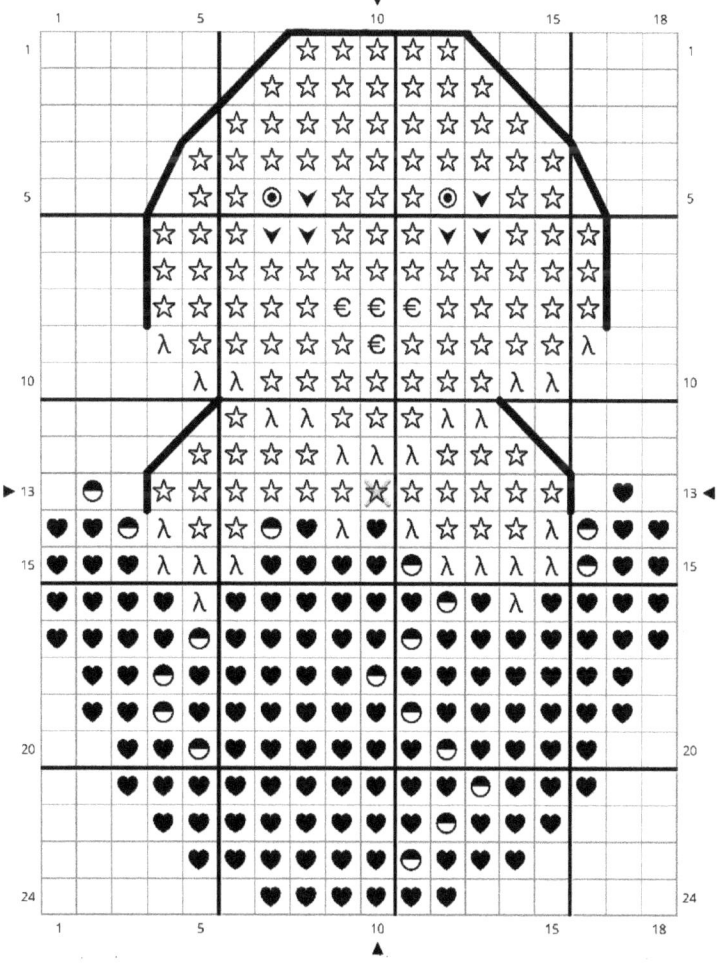

10 - Yellow Lily

General Information

Fabric count: 14 count Aida

Stitches: 28 by 28

Total skeins: 6

Finished size: 2" by 2"

Total Stitches: 517

Floss type: DMC

DMC Embroidery Floss Color Code

δ	D21	Alizarian LT	Stitches: 10
☆	D307	Lemon	Stitches: 254
Σ	D367	Pistachio Green DK	Stitches: 74
♡	D368	Pistachio Grenn LT	Stitches: 61
€	D445	Lemon LT	Stitches: 59
#	D3821	Straw	Stitches: 59

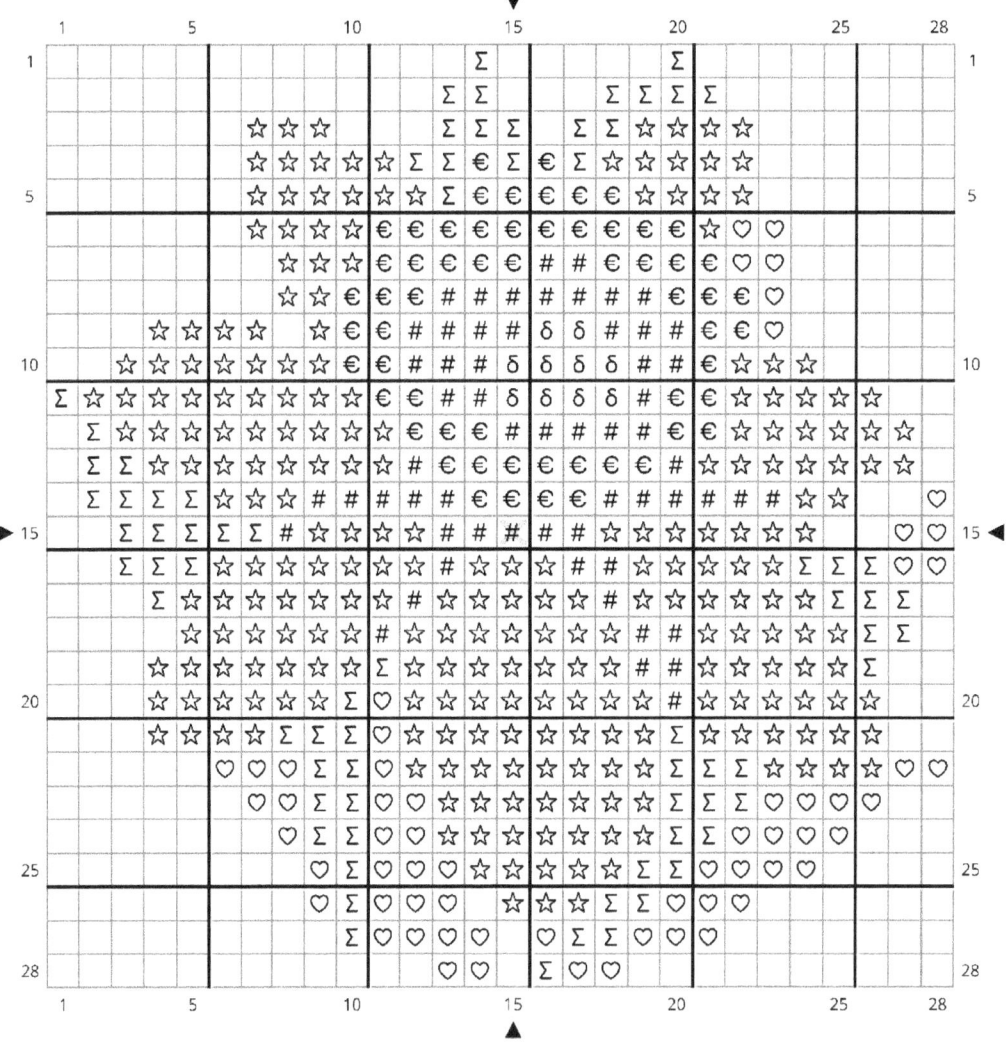

11 - Easter Basket

General Information

Fabric count: 14 count Aida

Stitches: 21 by 25

Total skeins: 9

Finished size: 1.5" by 1.7"

Total Stitches: 434

Floss type: DMC

DMC Embroidery Floss Color Code

▲	D07	Driftwood	Stitches: 189
╱	D09	Cocoa VY DK	Stitches: 83 Backstitching
#	D16	Chartreuse LT	Stitches: 2
▾	D307	Lemon	Stitches: 21
⋰	D307	Lemon	Stitches: 6 Backstitching
Σ	D700	Bright Green	Stitches: 28
Ω	D740	Tangerine	Stitches: 4
╱	D891	Carnation DK	Stitches: 27 Backstitching
♡	D957	Pale Geranium	Stitches: 57
◑	D996	Electric Blue MD	Stitches: 14
╱	D996	Electric Blue MD	Stitches: 3 Backstitching

Back Stitching

╱ **Basket's weave:** D09 Cocoa VY DK

⋰ **Yellow egg:** D307 Lemon

╱ **Bow:** D891 Carnation DK

╱ **Blue egg:** D996 Electric Blue MD

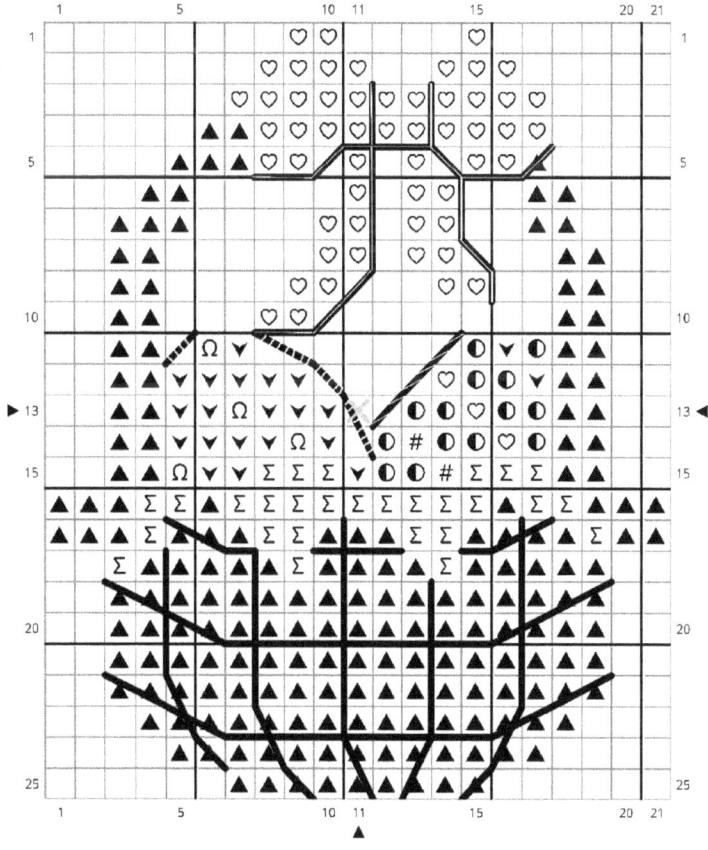

12 - Small Brown Bunny

General Information

Fabric count: 14 count Aida

Stitches: 21 by 29

Total skeins: 9

Finished size: 1.5" by 2"

Total Stitches: 351

Floss type: DMC

DMC Embroidery Floss Color Code

▛	D01	White Tin	Stitches: 93
◇	D07	Driftwood	Stitches: 140
€	D09	Cocoa VY DK	Stitches: 10
╱	D09	Cocoa VY DK	Stitches: 6 Backstitching
#	D16	Chartreuse LT	Stitches: 7
λ	D151	Dusty Rose VY LT	Stitches: 42
☆	D310	Black	Stitches: 2
♡	D957	Pale Geranium	Stitches: 36
╱	D957	Pale Geranium	Stitches: 4 Backstitching
◑	D996	Electric Blue MD	Stitches: 5
▼	DBLANC	White	Stitches: 6

Back Stitching

Eyebrows: D09 Cocoa VY DK

Mouth: D957 Pale Geranium

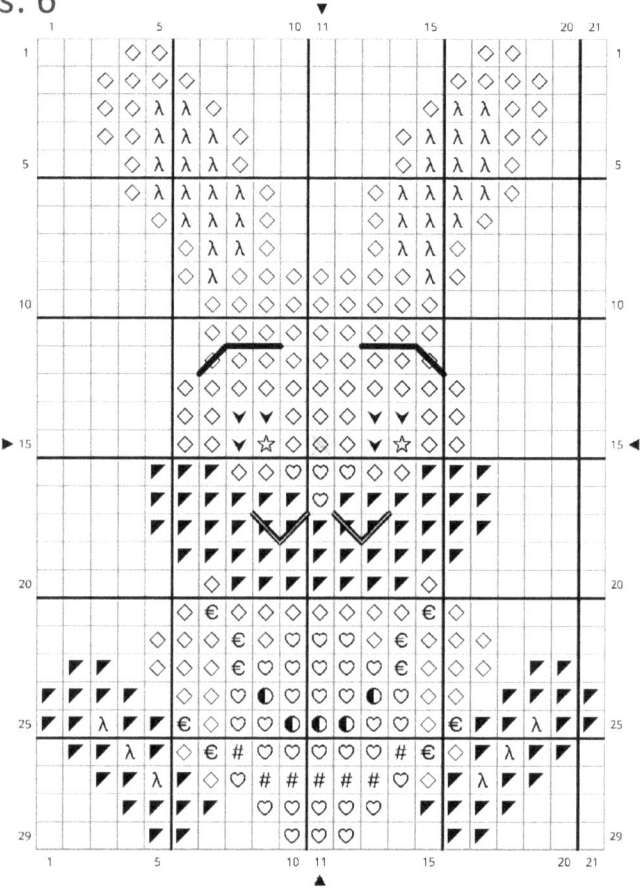

13 - Easter Cross

General Information

Fabric count: 14 count Aida

Stitches: 17 by 23

Total skeins: 10

Finished size: 1.2" by 1.6"

Total Stitches: 275

Floss type: DMC

DMC Embroidery Floss Color Code

▲	D07	Driftwood	Stitches: 89
€	D16	Chartreuse LT	Stitches: 4
λ	D28	Eggplant MD LT	Stitches: 38
%	D307	Lemon	Stitches: 6
Σ	D700	Bright Green	Stitches: 41
╱	D700	Bright Green	Stitches: 77 Backstitching
@	D740	Tangerine	Stitches: 4
♡	D957	Pale Geranium	Stitches: 4
◑	D996	Electric Blue MD	Stitches: 4
#	D3821	Straw	Stitches: 4
▼	DBLANC	White	Stitches: 4

Back Stitching

Leaves: D700 Bright Green

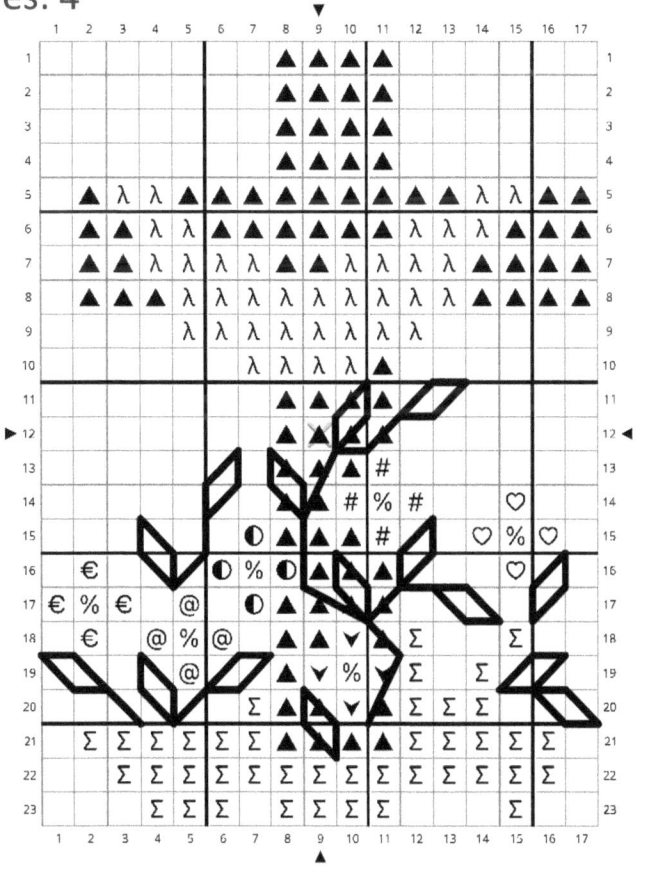

14 - "He is Risen"

General Information

Fabric count: 14 count Aida

Stitches: 26 by 21

Total skeins: 7

Finished size: 1.8" by 1.5"

Total Stitches: 158

Floss type: DMC

DMC Embroidery Floss Color Code

♡	D16	Chartreuse LT	Stitches: 12
◁	D210	Lavender MD	Stitches: 12
Ω	D307	Lemon	Stitches: 15
╱	D310	Black	Stitches: 83 Backstitching
δ	D740	Tangerine	Stitches: 12
£	D891	Carnation DK	Stitches: 12
◖	D996	Electric Blue MD	Stitches: 12

Back Stitching – "He is Risen": D310 Black

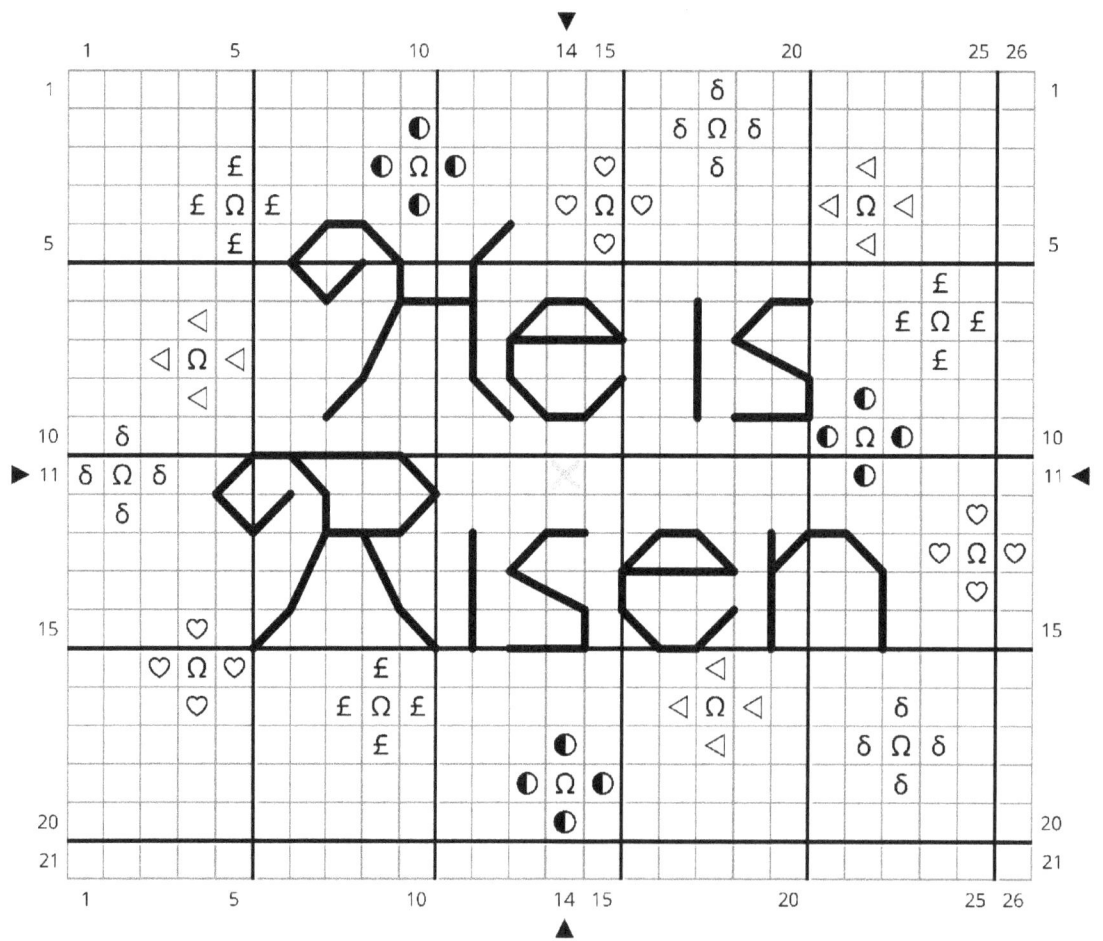

15 - Yellow Chick with Bow

General Information

Fabric count: 14 count Aida

Stitches: 28 by 25

Total skeins: 6

Finished size: 2" by 1.7"

Total Stitches: 390

Floss type: DMC

DMC Embroidery Floss Color Code

♥	D151	Dusty Rose VY LT	Stitches: 8
&	D307	Lemon	Stitches: 306
@	D310	Black	Stitches: 2
/	D310	Black	Stitches: 19 Backstitching
£	D740	Tangerine	Stitches: 4
µ	D891	Carnation DK	Stitches: 31
λ	D3821	Straw	Stitches: 20

Back Stitching – Feet: D310 Black

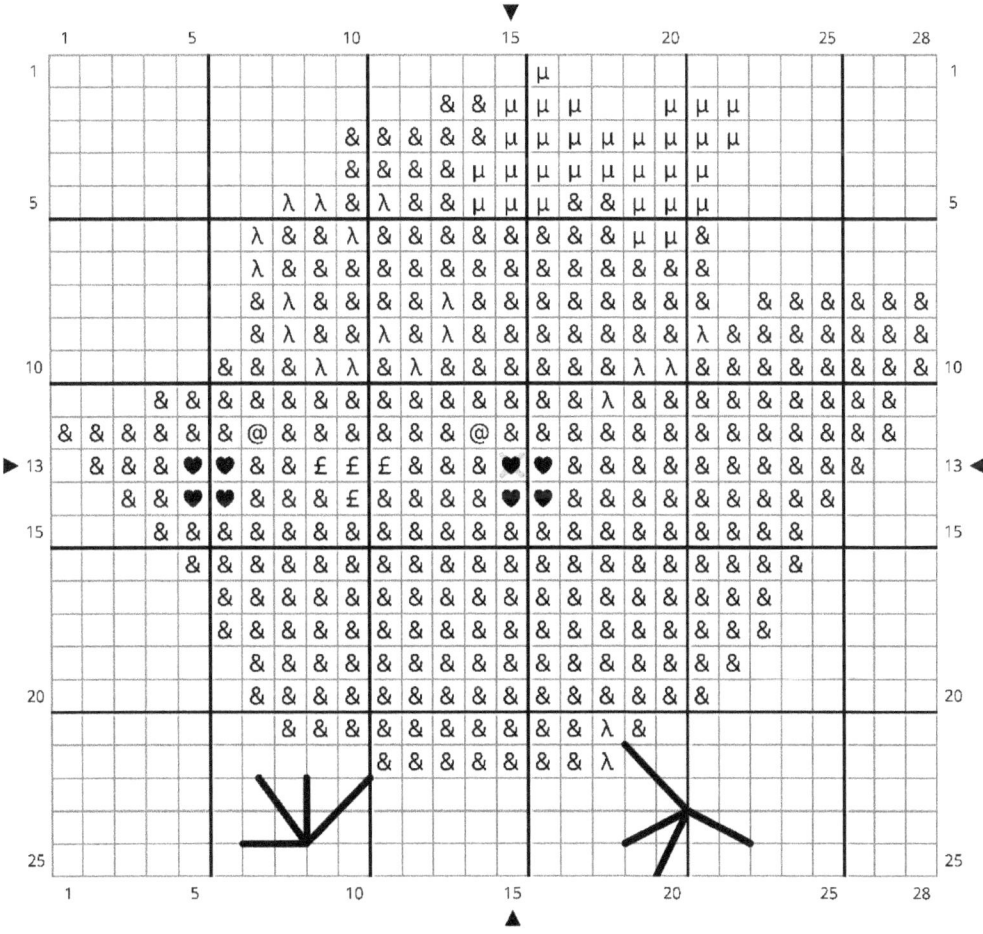

16 - Pink Flower

General Information

Fabric count: 14 count Aida

Stitches: 25 by 16

Total skeins: 6

Finished size: 1.7" by 1.1"

Total Stitches: 283

Floss type: DMC

DMC Embroidery Floss Color Code

☆	D307	Lemon	Stitches: 9
@	D367	Pistachio Green DK	Stitches: 55
φ	D368	Pistachio Green LT	Stitches: 14
π	D891	Carnation DK	Stitches: 35
/	D891	Carnation DK	Stitches: 37 Backstitching
♥	D894	Carnation VY LT	Stitches: 126
&	D3821	Straw	Stitches: 7

Back Stitching – Flower Petal Border: D891 Carnation DK

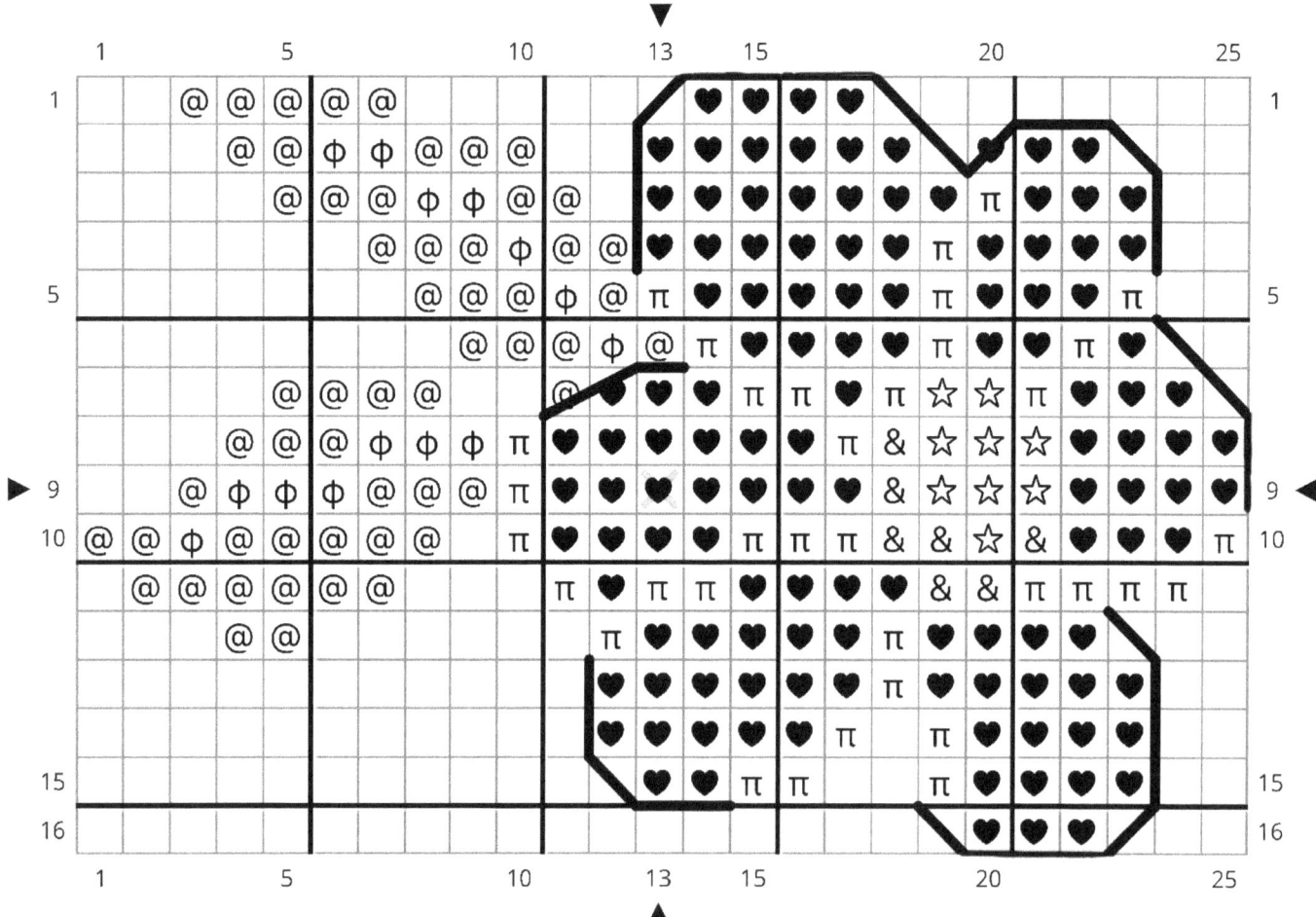